#4379

What Are You Figuring Now?

A Story about Benjamin Banneker

by Jeri Ferris
illustrations by Amy Johnson

HARCOURT BRACE & COMPANY
Orlando   Atlanta   Austin   Boston   San Francisco   Chicago   Dallas   New York
Toronto   London

What Are You Figuring Now?

For my son Mark,
who is a mathematician too

The author wishes to thank Silvio A. Bedini, Smithsonian Institution, Washington, D.C., for his help in providing background and scientific information from his own extensive research for this story of Benjamin Banneker's remarkable life and accomplishments.

This edition is published by special arrangement with Carolrhoda Books, Inc.

Grateful acknowledgment is made to Carolrhoda Books, Inc., Minneapolis, MN, for permission to reprint *What Are You Figuring Now? A Story about Benjamin Banneker* by Jeri Ferris, illustrated by Amy Johnson. Text copyright © 1988 by Jeri Ferris; illustrations copyright © 1988 by Carolrhoda Books, Inc.

Printed in the United States of America

ISBN 0-15-302227-2

1 2 3 4 5 6 7 8 9 10   011   97 96 95 94 93

Table of Contents

Chapter One

In 1736, when wolves and wildcats (and the king of England) owned the Maryland woods, most folks lived on farms. Most of them didn't have clocks or watches or appointment books. They knew what day it was by looking at the almanac. They knew what time it was by looking at the sun.

On the Banneky farm in northern Maryland, it was three o'clock by the sun, and Benjamin Banneky was out working in the tobacco field.

He heard the birds singing sleepily in the hickory trees. He knew the wolves and the wildcats were taking naps over in the woods. That's just what I'd like to do, thought Benjamin, feeling tired and hot and sticky. But instead he peered at another tobacco plant and picked the caterpillars off its wide leaves; . . . 57, 58, 59, he counted, as he dropped the caterpillars into a bag.

Benjamin was only five, but his Grandma Molly had already taught him hundreds of numbers. Benjamin loved to count. He counted whatever he saw, and he remembered how much he'd counted. This came in handy if anyone wanted to know how many caterpillars he'd found that morning or how many weeds he'd pulled the day before.

Benjamin also loved to listen to Grandma Molly's stories. He never got tired of hearing about her old home in England and how she had been sent across the ocean to America.

That evening, in the one-room cabin that Benjamin's family shared with Grandma Molly, she told Benjamin's favorite story again.

When Molly was a girl in England, she had milked cows for a farmer. One day, the cow she was milking kicked over its bucket of milk. Before Molly could do anything, the milk soaked into the dirt floor and was gone. The farmer thought that Molly had stolen the milk, so he sold her to a farmer in America. She would have to work seven years to pay for that bucket of spilled milk.

Molly crossed the ocean, worked her seven years, and was set free in Maryland when she was 21. She kept working and saved her money until she had enough to buy a little farm of her own, way out in the woods. She needed help to run the farm, so she bought a strong black slave named Banneky. But Banneky wasn't a slave for long because Molly soon gave him his freedom. Before long, the tall African man and the short English woman were married, and they built the fine cabin where Benjamin was sitting right now. Benjamin's mother, Mary, was born on Grandma Molly's farm. That's where his mother married his father, Robert, and that's where Benjamin and his sisters were born, too.

Benjamin watched his father's face as he listened to Grandma Molly's story. Benjamin's father had once been a slave, like Grandpa Banneky, and his owner had set him free. In fact, although most of the black people in Maryland were slaves, Benjamin and all of his family were free.

Benjamin wiped his bowl clean with the last of the corn bread and took a long drink of milk. Through the open door, he saw hundreds of stars twinkling at him. He wondered how many stars there were. Then he remembered something important, and he proudly told Grandma Molly how many caterpillars he had counted that day.

Grandma Molly smiled at him, her thin blond hair almost white in the firelight. "Benjie," she said, "I wonder what is left here for you to count."

The next week, bug-picking time was over. The tobacco plants were cut and hung up to dry. Then Benjamin had different jobs to do, such as moving the cows from place to place and picking the corn. Every evening, he studied with Grandma Molly. He learned to write with a goose-quill pen, and he learned to read from the only book Grandma Molly had—the Bible.

By the time spring came, Benjamin could write his ABCs with only a few ink blots. He tried to make fancy curlicues with the scratchy pen, the way Grandma Molly did, but his pen got stuck in the rough paper. He tried to read smoothly from the Bible, the way Grandma Molly did, but his tongue got stuck on the hard words. Grandma Molly just smiled. You're only six, she told him.

Then one day, Mr. Banneky said that Benjamin could go into town with him to buy something special—so special that it would take all the tobacco note money they had been saving. Benjamin wondered what could be so important. He did know that Grandma Molly's cabin, fine as it was, was becoming too small for the Bannekys' growing family. But Mary and Robert Banneky had saved their tobacco notes year after year for more than just a new cabin. Robert Banneky, a free black man, wanted to buy his *own* land.

On March 10, 1737, Benjamin, his father, and Grandma Molly drove to Joppa, the nearest Maryland town with government offices. Mr. Banneky stopped the horse in front of a small wooden building. Inside, Benjamin watched as his father bought one hundred acres of land right next to Grandma Molly's farm. He paid for the land with notes for seven thousand pounds of tobacco, and he told the man who wrote it all down to put Benjamin's name on the paper.

There it was, on the deed: "Robert Bannaky and Benjamin Bannaky his son...forever, one hundred acres of land..." The name was spelled wrong, but the land was theirs.

Now Benjamin didn't have as much time to

practice his reading and writing with Grandma Molly. He had more farm work to do instead. First he helped his father and mother plant the spring corn, and even Benjamin couldn't count all the kernels they put in the soft, rich earth. Then carefully, very carefully, they planted the tiny tobacco seeds in the ground Benjamin's father had prepared. Benjamin couldn't count them, either.

But in the fall, Benjamin counted the logs as he helped his father build a cabin on their new land. He counted the boards that made the roof. He counted the stones that made the fireplace. He counted the rooms—a big one downstairs and a little one upstairs. He counted the openings for windows. And he counted the heavy wooden shutters his father made to close over the window openings.

When he wasn't busy counting or helping with the tobacco plants, Benjamin spent his time fishing and hunting. He learned how to catch catfish, rockfish, shad, and eels in the river. He learned how to hunt ducks, deer, rabbits, and turkeys in the woods.

Life was good and the table was full. There was only one problem.

Benjamin wanted to know more than farming and fishing. He practiced reading from Grandma Molly's Bible every evening, but he wanted other books, too. And he wanted to count everything, everywhere.

Chapter Two

One day in November, Mrs. Banneky cooked a fine stew from a fat rabbit that Benjamin and his father had caught. She put bowls of hominy, carrots, and turnips on the table by the candles she had made out of bayberries. There was even a plate of honeycomb from the beehive in the orchard. It was a special meal because there was special news for Benjamin.

A Quaker farmer had moved into the next valley, and he planned to start a school that would be open during the winter when he wasn't farming. The Bannekys knew that Benjamin would be eager to go to school, where there would be books to read, facts to learn, and even more numbers to count and figure. They would be proud to have Benjamin go, said his father.

But before Benjamin could go to school, he had to have proper school clothes. So his mother and Grandma Molly wove some cloth, cut out a coat and pants, and stitched for days. Benjamin helped by gathering the eggs and milking the cows every day after his own chores were done. At last, the clothes were ready.

The first day of school, Benjamin did his chores early. Then he put on his new white shirt and other school clothes. When he was ready, his mother gave him a kiss. Grandma Molly gave him her best quill pen, a penknife to sharpen it with, and a kiss.

Benjamin waved to his family and raced down the hill and across the valley to the Quaker school. He passed squirrels, rabbits, and deer, and for once, he didn't stop to count them.

"Welcome," said the schoolmaster when Benjamin appeared at the door. "Won't thee come in?"

Benjamin counted 10 other students sitting on the benches. Some had rosy white faces like his Grandma Molly's. Some had dark brown faces like his. And there were books on the shelves!

Before Benjamin could count the books, the schoolmaster showed him where to sit and gave him a little board with a handle. "This is thy hornbook, Benjamin. See if thee can read it."

Benjamin had never seen a hornbook before. It didn't look like a book at all, he thought. On the square board was a piece of paper, and the paper was covered with a thin, transparent layer of horn to protect it. He could read the alphabet and the words on the paper right through the horn, and when his teacher came by, Benjamin read them out loud.

That afternoon, Benjamin hurried across the valley, up the hill, and into Grandma Molly's cabin. He proudly held out two arithmetic books. "The schoolmaster said I can take books home every day and that I can read as many books as I want to!"

Benjamin was surprised to see tears in his grandmother's eyes. "Benjie," she said, "I wonder what great things you're going to do some day. And I wonder how you can do them on a tobacco farm."

Now there weren't enough hours in the day or the night. Benjamin ran down the hill and across the valley to school every morning, all winter long. And every day, he soaked up learning the way dry ground soaks up rain.

On the way home, Benjamin would always stop to see Grandma Molly and show her his new books. Then he would dash off to do his chores. At last, after his mother had served supper from the big iron pot hanging over the fire, Benjamin would have time to read.

By the time Benjamin had gone to school for four winters, he had learned all the arithmetic, geography, and spelling his Quaker schoolmaster could teach him. Benjamin was almost grown up now, and since his father wasn't very well, it was up to him to do most of the farm work. This took every hour of every day, so Benjamin's school days were over.

Benjamin was proud of his farm. He was prouder still to be a free black man. But planting, weeding, watering, and picking bugs off tobacco leaves wasn't what he wanted to do all his life.

Benjamin knew he had to do something else— but what?

Chapter Three

For several years, Benjamin planted and weeded and watered. He helped his neighbors when they needed to write letters or figure their bills. Benjamin still loved numbers. To keep his mind busy, he made up complicated math puzzles using numbers and plants and animals.

In 1751, Benjamin was 20 years old. He stood straight and he walked proudly. In fact, before Grandma Molly died, she told Benjamin he looked as much like an African prince as his Grandpa Banneky had.

That fall, as usual, Benjamin rode to the nearby

trading town of Elkridge Landing for supplies. His horse trotted as fast as a horse can trot, but it wasn't fast enough for Benjamin. He couldn't wait to get to the end of the bumpy dirt road that wound through the tree-covered hills and buy the things his mother wanted. Then he could have a good, long talk with the folks in town. The truth was, as much as Benjamin loved his mother and father and three sisters, what he really enjoyed was talking about books or math problems or what was happening in other parts of the colonies. And as much as his mother and father and sisters loved Benjamin, they didn't quite know what to think of him.

It was about 10 o'clock by the sun when Benjamin tied his horse outside the store and pushed the door open. He tucked his hat under his arm, ordered a bolt of white cloth for his mother, and looked around for someone to talk to.

He saw a man he knew sitting by the salt barrel. Benjamin's heart jumped like a rabbit when he saw what the man had in his hand. It was a gold watch! Benjamin had always wanted to figure out how clocks and watches worked. In fact, every time he came to town, he studied the tall clock in the store, but he had never held a watch.

The man saw Benjamin staring at the gold watch. "Good morning," he said as Benjamin walked over, "do you have a new math puzzle today? I never did figure out the last one!" Benjamin laughed, and then he sat down for a good talk.

Late that afternoon, Benjamin rode home, slowly. He didn't want to harm the watch that his friend had let him borrow. It was wrapped in some of his mother's white cloth and tucked way down in his pocket. Even so, Benjamin thought he could hear the watch ticking steadily, echoing his own heartbeat.

That night after supper, Benjamin carefully laid the watch on the rough wooden table. His three sisters watched from the other side of the table. His mother sat by the fire, making a shirt for Benjamin out of the new white cloth, while his father finished a wooden stool he had started that morning.

Molly, Benjamin's littlest sister, couldn't sit still. "Benjamin, what are you doing? Where'd you get that pretty thing?"

Benjamin pulled the candle closer. "This is a watch," he said. "A man in town lent it to me, and now I'm going to take it apart and draw

the pieces. Then I'll put it back together again."
Benjamin held his breath and gently took the
back off the watch.

Every evening for a week, Benjamin sat at the
table with the watch, a candle, his quill pen and
ink, and paper. He copied each tiny wheel and
gear and pin. He memorized how they fit together
and how the watch worked. When the week was
up, he put the pieces back together and returned
the watch to its owner. Then Benjamin got a
good night's sleep.

The next day when the farm work was done,
Benjamin went into the woods. His feet crunched
the crisp red and orange leaves covering the
ground as he looked for just the right pieces of
wood. Not too old, not too dry, not too green,
not too soft. Just right.

That night, he sharpened Grandma Molly's old
penknife, spread out the drawings he'd made of
the watch, and started carving one of the pieces
of wood. Benjamin had chosen the hardest wood
he could find, and he had to stop again and
again to sharpen his knife. His sisters watched
and tried not to wiggle. When they asked what
he was doing, Benjamin just smiled. "Wait and
see," he said.

For two years, Benjamin farmed all day and worked on his wood pieces at night. Sometimes a piece broke, no matter how carefully he carved. Sometimes the wood was too green and curled up, no matter how carefully he chose the pieces. Then Benjamin had to start that piece all over again.

On one of his trips to Elkridge Landing, Benjamin bought small pieces of brass and iron from the blacksmith. He added these to his pile of wood pieces.

In 1753, two years after he had borrowed the gold watch, Benjamin put all the pieces together. He remembered just how each one had fit into the next one in the watch. When he was finished, they fit perfectly, like the pieces of a puzzle. He built a case, put the gears and wheels and pins inside just so, and added a bell made of iron. Benjamin had made his *own* clock.

From that day on, Benjamin knew exactly what time it was whether the sun was shining or not. In fact, he knew exactly what time it was even in the middle of the darkest night because the iron bell in his clock struck the hours.

Benjamin's neighbors heard about his wooden clock. They came to see it and listen to it and talk to the 22-year-old farmer who had made it. People in Elkridge Landing heard about the clock, and they came to see it. People in Joppa heard about the clock, and *they* came to see it.

Unfortunately, Benjamin didn't have time to talk about his clock. He had more work to do than ever. His father was not strong enough to do any farm work. There was no one to help Benjamin take care of the one-hundred-acre farm, with its tobacco, corn, wheat, fruit trees, horses, cows, and bees.

In 1759, Robert Banneky died. Now the farm belonged to Benjamin. His sisters had grown up, married, and moved to homes of their own, and only his mother was left. She still laughed and sang as she worked in the garden. She made candles as fast as Benjamin could use them, and she sewed new white shirts for him to wear. Benjamin farmed, taught himself to play the violin and the flute, and made up harder and harder math puzzles in his head. When he had time, he would ride into town to buy supplies and hear the latest news about what was happening in the other colonies.

But most of the time, Benjamin was alone. There were few black people around, and most of them were slaves. The white people Benjamin talked to in town all liked him and knew he was somebody special, but they weren't ready to be best friends with a black man, free or not.

Chapter Four

Benjamin heard the wooden clock strike six just as the morning sun peeked through the trees. It was 1771, and Benjamin was 40 years old. He still lived with his mother in the cabin on the hill. Some strangers had moved into the Hollow, and Benjamin was curious to see what they were building. Now that he had finished the spring planting, he could do just that. He saddled his horse and galloped off.

Soon he left the dirt road and pushed through branches and bushes, making his way down the hill into the Hollow. Before he reached the bottom, Benjamin heard shouts and hammering and roaring water. His horse pricked up its ears and trotted a little faster.

Through the trees, Benjamin saw a stable with enough stalls for—he counted again to be sure—80 horses. There were small shacks nearby, where the workers lived, and a huge mill was going up near the waterfall on the Patapsco River.

Benjamin rode closer. The men in charge wore the same dark coats and broad-brimmed hats he remembered from his Quaker schoolmaster. Benjamin looked down at his own coat. He, too, had usually worn plain Quaker clothing ever since then.

"Welcome," one of the men called. "Might thee be Benjamin Banneker, the man who made the wooden clock?" (Once he was an adult, Benjamin had decided to use the name *Banneker* instead of *Banneky.*)

Benjamin's heart leaped with the same excitement he'd felt 20 years ago when he'd built his own clock. Here, he was sure, were men like himself—men who liked to build and plan and figure. He jumped off his horse and walked over to shake hands.

When Benjamin rode home late that afternoon, he could hardly believe his good fortune. These men, the Ellicott brothers, were going to live only a few miles from his own farm. They planned to build a mill so big that all the farmers from miles around could bring their wheat there to be ground. And the best news of all was that they liked to talk about books and math problems and what was happening in the colonies.

Benjamin wanted to help the Ellicotts build the mill, and he wanted to talk about the colonies— why was King George sending soldiers to America from England, and why had his soldiers in their red coats shot some people in Boston, and why...? On the other hand, he had a one-hundred-acre farm to run.

Before long, the Ellicotts started a store in the Hollow and brought in newspapers and supplies from Baltimore, 10 miles away. Folks came from miles around to sit in the Ellicotts' store and talk. Benjamin and his mother brought eggs, honey, fruit, and vegetables to the store to trade for paper, ink, sugar, cloth, and molasses. And whenever Benjamin had a spare minute, he would join the conversation.

In December 1773, news came from Boston that some men had dumped three shiploads of British tea into Boston Harbor. The American colonists had decided not to buy any more tea from England until King George stopped taxing them and started listening to their complaints. They thought that the king was not ruling the colonies wisely, and they were tired of being ordered around by British soldiers.

King George didn't listen to the colonists. Instead, he sent more soldiers. In the spring of 1775, the first shots of the revolutionary war were fired at Lexington and Concord between American minutemen and British redcoats.

One year later, in 1776, the new American congress in Philadelphia decided, at last, that the colonies should be free from England. They didn't want a king across the sea to rule them anymore. Thomas Jefferson wrote the Declaration of Independence to tell the world that since King George had not treated his 13 American colonies fairly, they were now free and independent united states. (Or they would be, as soon as the American soldiers beat the British soldiers.)

But King George wanted to keep his American colonies. He sent more soldiers, and the revolutionary war went on and on.

Benjamin's farm was far from the fighting, but the American soldiers needed food. Benjamin planted more wheat and less tobacco, so he could send wheat to the army. And he read Thomas

Jefferson's words in the Declaration of Independence over and over again: "All men are created equal . . ."

In 1783, the Americans and the British signed a peace treaty. Benjamin was 52 years old, and he was proud to live in the new United States of America. There was just one question that puzzled him. If the United States was a free country, then why were some Americans still slaves? Benjamin didn't know the answer, but he kept the question in the back of his mind.

Now Benjamin was alone. His mother had died before the war was over, and she was buried in the family graveyard. He often thought of his mother and his father and Grandma Molly when he sat in the stillness of his cabin. But Benjamin didn't have much time to be lonely.

Andrew Ellicott's son George was studying surveying so he could measure land and make roads. A surveyor found the exact shape and boundaries of a piece of land by measuring distances and angles and figuring with geometry and trigonometry. Surveying wasn't easy to learn, but fortunately, young George knew Benjamin Banneker. Benjamin had so much math stored up in his head that he could help George whenever he was stuck on a problem. Along the way, Benjamin learned how to survey.

A surveyor had to understand astronomy—the study of the sun, moon, stars, planets, and comets —to accurately place the first line for whatever was being surveyed. When George began to study astronomy, he asked Benjamin for help with the math once again. Along the way, Benjamin learned astronomy, too.

In February 1788, George lent Benjamin his astronomy books and instruments; a smooth, sturdy table to put them on; and a new candle holder. Benjamin put the table under the window in his cabin. Then he opened the case of instruments. There, lying on soft, red velvet were a gleaming telescope and drafting tools.

Benjamin put the telescope to his eye and looked at the stars. The only sound was the ticking of his wooden clock. Hours later, when the last star had faded into the early morning, he carefully laid the telescope back in its case. Now Benjamin knew what else he wanted to do with his life. He, farmer and clock-maker, would become an astronomer.

The trouble was, astronomers look at the sky at night. Farmers are supposed to sleep at night.

And Benjamin wanted to be an astronomer *and* a farmer.

So Benjamin farmed all day long. After a nap, he would read his new astronomy books by candlelight and study the stars all night long. He made precise notes and drawings with his quill pen, using the drafting tools from George and all the mathematics he knew.

With all he had to do, Benjamin still read from two other books every day: Grandma Molly's Bible and the almanac. Most families had a Bible, and *every* family needed an almanac. It was the clock and calendar and doctor and storyteller of every home. The most important part of the almanac told when the sun and moon would rise and set, when there would be an eclipse, when there would be a full moon, and what the weather would be. Benjamin thought about all the figuring that went into an almanac, and he had an idea. He thought he could compute these figures as well as any almanac-maker and better than most. He decided to make an almanac himself.

For practice, Benjamin predicted an eclipse of the sun. After many nights of figuring with his compass and ruler and drawing the movement of the sun and the moon, he sent a copy of his drawings, measurements, and figures to George Ellicott. Then he put on his hat and hurried out to catch up on the farm work.

A few days later, a rider galloped up the road to Benjamin's door and handed him a letter from George. "I am astonished that you were able to make this prediction without anyone to teach you!" George wrote. Benjamin smiled and went back to his weeding.

By the end of the summer, Benjamin knew how to predict eclipses of the sun and of the moon. He could do all the figuring needed for an almanac, and he was ready to begin one of his own. But before Benjamin could get started, he had an unexpected adventure.

Chapter Five

By 1790, the revolutionary war had been over for 7 years and the Declaration of Independence was 14 years old, but the new United States still had no capital. So President George Washington chose a spot for the city right in the middle of the 13 states, in the woods overlooking the Potomac River. He chose Frenchman Pierre L'Enfant to plan just where the streets and buildings would look best, and he ordered the survey for the new city to begin in 1791.

The surveyor had to lay out the straight lines for the 10-square-mile city. He had to plot a perfect line running north and south using the stars, his instruments, his astronomical clock, and his calculations. Then he had to cross it with a perfect line running east and west. The United States

Capitol was to be built on the hill where the two lines crossed.

Major Andrew Ellicott, George Ellicott's cousin, was chosen to be the chief surveyor. But Major Ellicott needed help. He needed someone who knew astronomy and surveying. He needed someone who knew math and figuring. He needed someone who knew clocks. In short, he needed Benjamin Banneker.

President Washington and Thomas Jefferson, the secretary of state, agreed that Benjamin Banneker was just the man to be the chief surveyor's chief assistant. Benjamin hoped to prove they were right.

He put aside his telescope and drafting tools, and he packed his best dark suit and white linen shirts. He added his quill pen, an ink bottle, and some paper, in case he had time to make notes for his almanac. Before he left, he asked his sisters and their husbands to look after his farm.

On a cold, rainy morning in early February 1791, when Benjamin was almost 60 years old, he and Major Ellicott set off on horseback to make camp in Alexandria, Virginia, about 40 miles away. They arrived, wet and cold, on the evening of February 7.

The next day, the two men rode to a hill outside the town to set up the observation tent, where Benjamin would work. Andrew Ellicott owned some of the finest astronomical instruments in the world, and Benjamin was to use them. He was in charge of the astronomical clock, three large telescopes, and many other tools used in surveying.

At last the survey began. Andrew took his crew of men and began chopping down trees so he could lay out straight lines for the city. Benjamin set up the largest and best telescope so that it pointed through an opening in the roof of the tent. That night, he began his observations of the stars as they crossed a certain point in the sky. He recorded each observation, figured out the exact latitude and longitude, and drew the base points for the lines Andrew would lay the following day.

When the stars faded, Benjamin had time for only a short nap. Soon he was up again to explain his figures to Andrew, to record observations of the sun, and to check the astronomical clock.

It rained a lot that spring, and it was cold at night in the tent. In fact, it was cold in the daytime, too, but Benjamin was too busy to mind.

If he ever had a spare minute, which wasn't often, he would use the time to work on his almanac.

On March 12, Benjamin's name was in the newspaper. The *Georgetown Weekly Ledger* reported that Andrew Ellicott was "attended by *Benjamin Banniker* . . . surveyor and astronomer." His name was spelled wrong again, but Benjamin carefully and proudly folded his copy of the newspaper and laid it aside with his notes.

That same month, Benjamin met the most famous man in the United States. President Washington himself came to visit the survey camp on March 28. Benjamin dressed in his best dark suit, his finest linen shirt, and a new three-cornered hat. He smiled when he heard someone in the crowd say that Mr. Banneker looked like Benjamin Franklin with brown skin.

When Benjamin bowed deeply before the tall president, he tried to feel as calm on the inside as he looked on the outside, but his heart felt like a runaway clock.

On April 15, Benjamin again dressed in his very best clothes. He stood with Andrew Ellicott and Pierre L'Enfant as the first stone marker was placed at Jones's Point. This marked the first corner of the capital city.

By late spring, Benjamin had finished his figures. After working night and day, seven days a week, he was ready to return to his farm. Before he left, Benjamin looked at L'Enfant's plans for the new city. They showed streets laid out like a checkerboard, with wide avenues spreading out from the Capitol like the spokes of a wheel. They also included plenty of parks and fountains. Benjamin thought the plans were just right.

As he walked to his horse, Benjamin thought about his three months as the chief surveyor's chief assistant. He felt proud that he, Benjamin Banneker, had helped to lay out the capital city of the United States. What an honor it had been! Then off he galloped. He had an almanac to write.

Chapter Six

Benjamin stopped at the Ellicotts' store on the way home to buy candles, ink, and paper. His neighbors saw him and hurried over to shake his hand and ask about his adventures.

Hours later, Benjamin shook the last hand and got back on his horse. In his bulging saddlebags were his suit, his notes, the newspaper with his name in it, and the new candles and ink from the store. Tucked away carefully was a brand-new, handsome book with three hundred blank pages of handmade paper. Benjamin planned to write his almanac on these fine pages.

At last he was home. When Benjamin opened the cabin door, he was greeted by the ticking of his wooden clock. The cabin was clean and neat. His sisters had taken good care of it and of his farm while he was gone.

Benjamin's heart beat faster as he thought about the almanac he planned to write. He opened his blank book, lit two candles, and took his telescope out of its case. The unpacking would have to wait until tomorrow.

Hours later, as the morning sky was turning pale blue in the east, Benjamin put the telescope away and stretched. Now he planned to take a good long rest—all day in fact.

For the first time in 40 years, Benjamin did not have one hundred acres to farm. The year before, he had sold most of his land to the Ellicotts. It was, Benjamin had decided, the answer to his problem. It seemed that being an astronomer *and* a farmer was one job too many. Now he had a little garden for vegetables, trees for fruit, bees for honey, and a cow for milk. It was just the right size farm for an astronomer.

But now it was already the end of April, and Benjamin wanted to have his almanac for 1792 done by the end of May. The clock ticked and the candles sputtered as Benjamin's pen scratched across the pages of his blank book, night after night and day after day. Every figure had to be exact: sunrise, sunset, moonrise, eclipses of sun and moon, rising and setting of the bright stars, position of the planets. Benjamin had to do at least 68 complicated math problems, by quill pen, just to figure each eclipse. He checked his figures over and over.

When all the figuring and drawing were done, Benjamin began the next step. At the top of a fresh sheet of paper, in his neatest and most elegant handwriting, he wrote "January 1st month hath 31 days." He listed the days in the month down the side and made headings for all of his figures, such as "sunrise" and "sunset," across the top. Hours later, the page for January was finished.

By the end of May, Benjamin's almanac for the year 1792 was complete. But would anyone want to print an almanac written by a black man who had been a farmer all his life?

Benjamin worked in his garden for the next few days while he thought about what to do. He rested under a big pear tree while he thought some more. Then he took some clean, blank pages and copied his almanac over four times.

He sent one of the copies to a printer in Georgetown, where the newspaper that had published the article about him had been printed. He talked to George Ellicott and gave him a copy to send to James Pemberton, a printer in Philadelphia. He put on his best dark waistcoat and broad-brimmed hat and galloped off to Baltimore to meet William Goddard, who published the *Maryland Journal.* He gave Goddard a copy. Then he hurried home and sent off another copy to Pemberton in Philadelphia. Pemberton had sent his first copy of Benjamin's almanac to the most important scientist in the United States, David Rittenhouse.

By July 1791, Benjamin was still waiting to hear from one of the printers—or better yet, from all of them. He mended the cow shed. He weeded the vegetable garden. He studied his bees as they flew in and out of their hives.

Meanwhile, news of Benjamin Banneker's accomplishments was spreading. Benjamin heard that his name was used in a Fourth of July speech in Baltimore. Quakers and abolition societies, both of whom opposed slavery, said his work was proof that black people were just as smart as white people.

Benjamin thought about all this while he waited to hear from the printers. He remembered that Jefferson had written the words "all men are created equal" in the Declaration of Independence.

Benjamin still didn't understand how some Americans could be slaves if everyone was equal.

He took out more paper and copied his almanac one more time. Then Benjamin began a letter to "Thomas Jefferson Secretary of State," in the elegant handwriting Grandma Molly had taught him. His words were elegant, too, as he gently reminded Jefferson of the evils of slavery. "Suffer me to recall to your mind" the war against England, he wrote, "a time in which you clearly saw the injustice of a State of Slavery." Then he reminded Jefferson of his own words, "We hold these truths to be self-evident, that all men are created equal . . ." Benjamin compared the slavery of Americans by England to the slavery of blacks by whites. Surely, he wrote, correction of one requires correction of the other. Was nothing to be done about America's slaves?

He finished by saying he was sending Mr. Jefferson "a copy of an Almanack which I have calculated for the Succeeding year." He reminded Jefferson that he, Benjamin Banneker, had taken part in the survey of the new capital city and signed the letter

Your most Obedient humble Servant
Benjamin Banneker

Benjamin's letter and the copy of the almanac arrived in Philadelphia, then the capital city, on August 26. Mr. Jefferson sat right down and read them.

On August 30, Jefferson wrote Benjamin a letter of thanks. He told him that he had sent the almanac to the Academy of Sciences at Paris, France, as proof of what American blacks could do. He signed it

I am with great esteem, Sir
your most obed^t humble serv^t.
Thomas Jefferson

Benjamin was pleased, very pleased. He put Mr. Jefferson's letter away with the newspaper that had his name in it. He would wait and hope that his letter to Mr. Jefferson would help abolish slavery.

After several months, Benjamin finally heard that William Goddard in Baltimore and James Pemberton in Philadelphia both wanted to print his almanac.

Now he had to put the tiny three-by-five-inch book together. Benjamin and the printers started collecting stories, poems, recipes, and remedies for ailments to fill up the pages not used by Benjamin's monthly figures.

Benjamin Banneker's Almanack for 1792 included a short article about Benjamin. The author of the article, Dr. James McHenry, said that the almanac was "fresh proof that the powers of the mind are [not connected to] the color of the skin."

The almanac was a complete success. Benjamin became even more famous than he had been before. Some people wrote to him, and others walked up the hill right to his door. His table was usually covered with books and papers, but he was never too busy to invite his guests in and make them feel at home.

Soon it was time to start on the figures for the 1793 almanac. Again, Benjamin stayed up late into the night, observing, drawing, and figuring to the nearest second. He also had letters to write and visitors to talk to. Benjamin had never been so happy.

Benjamin's almanac for 1793 was one of the most important books of the 1790s. It included Benjamin's letter to Thomas Jefferson and Jefferson's reply, as well as a speech by Sir William Pitt of England about stopping slavery. There was also a section by Dr. Benjamin Rush outlining his plan for a peace office. Dr. Rush said that since the United States had a war department, it should have a peace department, too.

In his 1794 almanac, Benjamin figured eclipses for London, England, as well as for the United States. He added charts showing when high and low tide would occur all up and down the Chesapeake Bay. He listed alphabetically 25 ports for ships, from the southern states to as far north as Quebec, Canada. The printer in Virginia said that his calculator was "that ingenious self-taught Astronomer, Benjamin Banneker, a black man."

On the cover of the almanac for 1795 was a woodcut portrait of Benjamin wearing Quaker clothes, as usual. The 1795 almanac was so popular that at least nine different printers made copies. People who bought it at the country store knew they could count on the figures to be right, and they liked the little stories, medical cures, riddles, and weather forecasts.

By 1797, at least 28 different versions of Benjamin Banneker's almanacs had been printed in six years. But then he stopped making almanacs. He didn't tell anyone why. He just stopped.

Maybe he had decided he'd rather wrap himself up in his warm cloak and lie out under the pear tree all night, watching the stars and their eternal marking of time.

AFTERWORD

Benjamin usually had his book of blank pages with him when he sat under the pear tree. He wrote about the weather. He wrote about what his bees did. He copied parts of the Bible into his book. Then he'd put on his broad-brimmed hat and hoe the corn and weed the garden.

He had lots of visitors, who wrote their names in a special guest book Benjamin kept. He traded math puzzles with other math lovers. He corrected mistakes in some of the books he used. And, of course, he stayed up every night to watch the stars.

In 1800, he predicted that there would be an eclipse on October 18 of that year. No other astronomer agreed, so Benjamin wrote "the mistake may be in me." On October 18, 1800, there *was* an eclipse.

Benjamin always kept an iron kettle simmering on the fire. In the morning, he would cut a large piece of salt pork and toss it in the kettle. In the afternoon, he would make cornmeal dumplings and add them to the kettle. In the evening, he would pick fresh vegetables from the garden and get fresh milk from the cow. Then he would have a feast.

Benjamin still played the flute and violin, and he sat under the pear tree in the evening, playing for himself and the stars. He went to the Quaker Meeting House for church. He went to the Ellicotts' store for shoes, salt pork, molasses, candles, and ink. And he took long walks, leaning on his cane, enjoying his fruit trees and bees and the woods all around.

October 9, 1806, was a crisp fall day. Benjamin went out for his morning walk, met a friend, and stopped to talk. Suddenly, Benjamin felt sick, and his friend helped him home. Benjamin looked at the sky one last time. He heard the ticking of his wooden clock one last time. Then his heart stopped, and he died.

On the day of Benjamin's funeral, his cabin burned to the ground. The wooden clock, the newspaper with Benjamin's name in it, the letter from Thomas Jefferson, and his copies of the almanacs were all destroyed. Only his Bible was left, because it had been used at his funeral.

Today, no one knows for sure where Benjamin's cabin was. No one knows for sure where he is buried. But we *do* know that Benjamin Banneker was a very special man, a free black man, a farmer, who built by hand a wooden striking clock, who was appointed by George Washington to help survey the city of Washington, D.C., who calculated his own almanacs, and who figured out for himself the mysteries of the stars, the planets, and time itself.

MORE ABOUT BENJAMIN BANNEKER

1. Benjamin's grandfather was originally called *Bannka* or *Bannaka*. Later, this became *Banneky* (sometimes misspelled *Bannaky*). Banneky's daughter, Mary Banneky, married Robert, who had no last name because he had been a slave. Robert took Mary's name and became Robert Banneky. Benjamin Banneky, their son, eventually changed his name to Benjamin Banneker.

2. Tobacco notes were given in exchange for tobacco leaves. The number of pounds of tobacco sold was written on the tobacco note, and the note was used as money.

3. The following is an example of one of Benjamin Banneker's math problems. (Answer on next page.)

A gentleman sent his servant with 100 pounds to buy 100 cattle [bullocks and cows] and sheep, with orders to give 5 pounds for each bullock, 20 shillings worth of cows, and 1 shilling for each sheep. What number of each sort did he buy for his master? *There are 20 shillings in a pound.*

4. George Ellicott's father and cousin were both named Andrew Ellicott.

5. In 1792, Pierre L'Enfant argued with the men in charge of building the new capital city. He was so angry that he returned to France in a huff, taking his plans for the city with him. It is likely, although no one knows for sure, that Benjamin Banneker and Andrew Ellicott worked together to replace the plans.

Answer to math problem:

$$
\begin{array}{rcr}
\text{19 bullocks at 5 pounds each} & = & \text{95 pounds} \\
\text{1 cow at 20 shillings} & = & \text{1 pound} \\
\text{80 sheep at 1 shilling each} & = & \underline{\text{4 pounds}} \\
& & \text{100 pounds}
\end{array}
$$

My Chemo Journey

This journal belongs to

_____

_____

_____